Innovation and emancipation of computerization

Shongwe Mbho

Published by Shongwe Mbhoshongwane Elmond, 2025.

INNOVATION AND EMANCIPATION OF COMPUTERIZATION

First edition. July 24, 2025.

ISBN: 979-8230963936

Written by Shongwe Mbho.

Also by Shongwe Mbho

Dancing in the Middle of a Marriage Storm
The intricacies in eswatini
tibongo netinanatelo
Emeswati Abetsini Atsini
Innovation and emancipation of computerization

One may ask a simple question; why so significant to dedicate this book to my late daughter, who was also my first child after my marriage? She was my born when I was so entrenched in computerization and when I was just about to resign from my first job that, I so loved not because of any problem but the desire to meet new challenges in the private sector of computerization in the country. Now, I had two new items that occupied my mind and that I loved dearly; my computerization work and my daughter. She laid a foundation to my continued love for information, communication and technology, processes I still admire todate.

There is nothing like automatic, GIGO, infinity, etc., functions of whatever operations are designed and programmed by the designer

AUTHOR : SHONGWE MBHO

A Systems Analyst, Computer Programmer, Senator (1998 - 2003), Political Commentator, Columnist, African Union Elections Observer Expert, Senator (1998 - 2003), an Author of "Emeswati Abetsini Atsini", "Dancing in the Middle of a Marriage Storm", "The Intricacies in Eswatini Politics Culture Development" and "Tibongo neTinanatelo" published online by www.Draft2Digital.com[1] and www.smashwords.com[2] I am one of the first Swazi trained computer programmers in the country and got involved with the early computerization of government operations. Currently designing electronic projects and entrenched in computerization and electronic usage I am well over 70 years old and my email address is mbhoshongwe@gmail.com and my contact cell number is +26876055551 and wasp number +26878282170

1. http://www.Draft2Digital.com

2. http://www.smashwords.com

FORWARD :

In an era where digital connectivity shapes the fabric of every society and nation, the transformative power of Information, Communication and Technology (ICT) can't be overstated. Eswatini, a nation rich in culture, tradition and custom, is also embracing the rapid advances of the digital age, striving to harness ICT to faster sustainable development, enhance good governance, and improve the quality of life for its citizens.

This book offers a comprehensive exploration of the journey of ICT in Eswatini, highlighting the milestones achieved, the challenges faced, and the opportunities that lie ahead. It provides valuable insights into how technology is reshaping sectors such as education, healthcare, agriculture, and business, contributing to the nation's vision of a digitally empowered society.

As we delve into stories, policies, innovations, and aspirations documented within these pages, it is my hope that readers will gain a deeper understanding of Eswatini's unique context and its unwavering commitment to leveraging ICT for national progress and development. May, this work inspire continued efforts towards building an inclusive digital future for Eswatini and the region.

Nolwazi G. Dlamini

INTRODUCTION :

There are things and or operations that are done repeatedly without any brain or mind challenges. Then, within this repeatedly processing, what would have been the function and purpose of the brain and mind power? It seems, both brain and mind are underutilized, not useful and delaying futuristic development plans, be they cultural, economic or political.

When God or any Super Being created everything His creation might need, even to reproduce, He sanctioned human beings to have domain of all creation. Is this happening, if not why not? Human beings are made or schooled to believe that can achieve this, but it seems use less than 5 percent of their brain power. They have the capacity, but they go for something less, may be due to ignorance of their own potentials. They simply push the problems to other people including government thus entrenching the blame syndrome an attitude that dominates their minds. Then, later introduced to handouts philosophy, thus cementing a permanent dependence on those in leadership.

According to the Holy Bible, human beings were made in the image of God and His likeliness, meaning that they have all the attributes of God but they aren't Him. He has the supreme power and His creation has power, if it weren't so, He would have remained here to teach them on daily basis of how to do their duties and responsibilities.

Human beings are quick to identify imbeciles amongst themselves, when in fact, according to their creation are imbeciles and have to take their rightful position of domination not over ourselves but the other creation of God. Who is the only source, as human beings?

Ignorance has dominated human being thoughts and ideas, hence underutilized their potentials to achieve their God given items and rights. Is technology going to succeed in awakening human beings from the slender since creation to appreciate and understand the innovation and emancipation of computerization? Technology development has afforded human beings new tools to function without their physical sweat, the emergences of the fourth industrial revolution (4IR) and quickly followed by the artificial intelligence (AI). Some may even think that technology is new, when in fact, it has always been there, but our failure to discover and benefit from it.

THE BOOK ITSELF :

At the end of every topic, there is a summary of that topic and the reader is expected to do the same and later submit to the provided email address. These comments will appear in the next version of the book. Off-course these comments will appear with the names of the commentators. This book gives a path of computerization in the country which was initiated by the Canadian government that later provided training programmers and systems analysts to some of the incoming, that is, would be computer Swazi experts and management in computerization for the government computer centre. This book has names of the first and second batch of Swazis who worked in this government computer centre; management, systems analysis and programming, computer operation, data capture, cleaners and government departments key contact persons. One may wonder, why cleaners; the computer room needed to be completely clean, air-condition, windows closed and thus dust free. Unfortunately, some of the people mentioned have passed on, may their souls rest in eternal peace.

INFORMATION AND THE MYTH OF AUTOMATIC :

Information has always been the key factor of survival, progress and development in the world over from the very beginning. Technology has always been the catalyst in major operations. One can imagine with amazement how the pyramids were built, cutting and moving the stones to all the levels until the top. This shows that technology is as old as creation itself.

Some countries and their peoples wanted get it first before others, hence take advantage and improve their existing logistics and strategies, that will appeal to the market and business demands of the time and in so doing creating permanent consumers around the world. Unfortunately, many countries have comfortably remained consumers of technology and its tools.

Those complex and probably difficult routes, systems and programs forced the first computer engineers, systems analysts and philosophers of the time, crafted names to silence others from further inquiring about how certain operations occur and their drivers that is, the reason human beings hear of automatic operation.

They produced programmed machines to do certain operations and referred to them as automatic machines, thus cutting any further questions and debates from other people and or others users. Even today, there are people out there who still believe in automatic operations of machines.

There is nothing like automatic, doing operations on its own, these machines are programmed to operate the way, they do, by a human being using technological skills. No country, no individuals to claim immunity from the claws of information, impact of information communication technology. This has changed the way people think and act.

- It may look amazing with sophisticated operations, as if it has its own original operations, no someone designed it and knows how it operates and fully understands the capacity and strength of it not being absorbed and understood by ordinary thinking, hence normal thinking will conclude that it is automatic. It be considered to have automatic to automatize the automatic.

THE DAWN OF COMPUTERIZATION AND THE FOUNDERS :

So, Eswatini couldn't escape this trend of performing things or items by using computation and technology. But before, putting this country on to the road map, one must first unpack where this technology came from or if indeed it migrated or the source of its origin; before, on or after creation of mankind and who was responsible for it, what was its purpose and who benefited from it, how has it penetrated into human being lives, knowingly or unknowingly, etc.? They have surrendered all their details into this technological innovation (TI)? Or are they going to technology with their old ways of processing data?

Our personal details are all over the technological divide and information about them and everything else is easily accessible and with faster than the twinkly of an eye and regardless of the distance apart, globally village indeed, a way of life.

But then, where do human beings come from and at what speed have they been moving? It is said that if you don't know where you are going, any way will lead you there. As human beings, are they aware of this saying? Then, what are they doing about it?

Or do they know the direction where they are going and it is said that they are going back to the future. It is like, they were once in the future. Yes, the world, countries and human beings and off-course other animals are moving but to where? They are looking for opportunities and better life styles for themselves.

The first computing machine by Countess Ada Lovelace introduced as computing engine capable of calculating and tabulating which later helped mathematicians like Charles Babbage and Louis Menebria to carry out their massive mathematical calculations, sparked the era of computation.

These two mathematicians had to build the computer and provide documentation of its operations and how it carries the calculations, that is, code programs that would verify the input, process the data and produce information in a report format.

Charles Babbage is known as the father of computers and needed a machine to carry out his massive mathematical calculations. He is known for his 1833 computer that created a foundation for the current innovation and technology of computers.

They are told that his initiative of coming up with a machine that would execute massive calculations, later helped the space exploration engineers and astronauts develop even more powerful machines to do this, hence the achievement of Apollo 11, in 1969, with two astronauts landing on the moon and one remaining in the main vehicle.

It can be noticed that computerization is about the hardware and software; the engine and the systems. Computerization was then in motion and new players and demands pushing new innovations to all directions and by the beginning of the 20th century that was in full swing, attracting not only mathematicians but the business world.

The International Business Machine (IBM) came and introduced the IBM 9AC, a name that was influenced by business gurus suggesting that financial management and auditing had a hand on its design and application. Then, IBM developed a large scale computerized accounting system with the manual document showing how the system functioned and later introduced the software in the market for the financial management and advisory skills, computing and software gurus to view it and this took place in the United States of America (US) which is the home country of IBM.

It be noted that Charles Babbage was British suggesting that Great Britain, indeed was also doing something on computerization and the computer experts and those interested in computer business were going from one continent to another, looking for opportunities and all associated with computerization.

The International Computers Limited (ICL) developed its own massive computer called 1900 and it too, quickly penetrated into the African continent. The Republic of South Africa was the first country to use it in the region and quickly landed in Eswatini in the early 1973s with the help of four Canadian experts; one in accounting and the three in systems designs, analysis and programming.

They came here to start and establish the government computer centre with the future role to computerize all government units, sections and departments and then their other tasks were to recruit and train Swazis, in systems designs, analysis and programming including operations and data capturing and or keying in.

The systems developed were; accounting, salaries, graded tax, motor vehicle registration, income tax, government vehicles, etc. Although, government was running under the Westminster repealed Independence Constitution, continued to embrace and endorse the usefulness of computerization.

- Challenges of having correct, easily accessible and ready for usage information, but being stored as achieves, implying that computerization had no meaning. Problems no matter how big or sophisticated may look like create further challenges in order to produce the desired solutions. Your desire is to eat the meat and the skinning the object shouldn't delay or frustrate your desire hence the idea of computerization.

ESTABLISHMENT OF COMPUTERIZATION IN ESWATINI :

By 1976 government of Eswatini computer systems were manned by Swazis, in coding, key punching, data capturing, dispatch, operations, programming, designs and analysis and including computer management, manager being Mathokoza D. Dlamini. It was one of the first localization the country achieved in such a new and uncommon type of work.

The first batch of eMeswati to be recruited and trained on the job as Programmers or Systems Analysts was in 1974; David D. Dlamini, Nathaniel H. Mahluza, Nelson B. Mayisela, Kenneth B. Manyatsi, Mathew N. Masondo and Elmond M. Shongwe.

Enock J. Simelane and Mbuso B. Khumalo had been recruited from within government structures, also true with Mathokoza D Dlamini and seconded to join the computer programming or systems analysis team and later sent to Canada for computer studies, but Mathokoza D. Dlamini to under start management from the experts. In order to communicate with the computers, one had to learn their languages and master their applications. Computer operators and data key-punchers or captures included, Tennyson Mabusela, Mphumelelo Hlophe, Petsi Zeeman and Aunty Mabuza.

The most common computer language used at the time was the Common Business Oriented Language (COBOL), although there were other languages like; Formula Translator (ForTran), Algorithm Oriented Language (Algol), Report Program Generator (RPG), Tabulation (TAB) and other utility software for handling file management in the machine, were used, like sorting, copying, etc.

Some of these Swazis were later sent to Canada for further studies. And in 1978 I resigned from government to join a private computer company, as its systems analyst, programmer and systems executive, becoming the first Swazi to occupy that position in that company.

By the end of 1975, other additional trainee programmers or systems analysts were recruited including computer operators and data key punchers or captures, thus facilitating others to go to Canada. At the time, government civil servants saw computers and their usage as a process to take away their jobs and for the fact that those recruited were young and not coming from the government structures and departments.

The government of Eswatini is indebted to the government of Canada, who supplied the specialists in accounting, systems analysts, designers, consultants and management to set up the base of computerization in the country and even provided scholarship for further training in Canada, on the job training and short courses in South Africa. Within three years, the government computer centre was running and manned by Swazis.

- Probably the first localization plan that was on target and achieved within timeframe. Eswatini, isn't a big country and at the time its population was below one million but didn't resist computerization that was sweeping across the world. And in a way, was going through the Constitutional crisis after the repeal of the Westminster Independence Constitution.

COMPUTER COMPANIES, OPERATING SYSTEMS AND NETWORKS :

Generally, computerization gained a huge ground in the 1970s, with the development of both software and hardware by a number of computer companies and even computer professionals. A Germany computer software application company, SAP, developed a large scale business software and by 1973, it released its first computerized financial management system in Germany.

Computerization had already gained ground in financial management and auditing even though it had its original function in mathematical applications.

Peacht Ree; another company publicly released its computerized financial management and auditing software in 1976, Atlanta United States of America and used IBM Personal computer platform, thus broadening the scope in the computerized financial and auditing industry.

This project was spearheaded by computer professionals who had worked for IBM and were keen to realize an improved computerized financial management and auditing systems. And these systems have been improving ever since, suggesting that the best such software is already in the market and or being redesigned to suit current financial management and auditing challenges.

So, one could become a software developer and or designer and or hardware specialists thus opening outsourcing avenues. Computerization has always been associated with accuracy, speed and efficiency, implying that it must replace a manual system that lacks these three tasks.

Computer development is best known by their generations and operation systems. They were built with the power to be switched off and on, either this built in them or out of them; the operation system. This would make the machine to start functioning or working and then respond to the user's programs.

Can one ever imagine, how we human beings function; sleep, wake up or never wake up, load the day's work in their sequence and other programs to remind us of other activities that need our attention and then reprogram our new day's work and activities.

But what is the source of energy in our bodies to do all these, is it built inside or outside of these bodies? And what happens if that energy source malfunction, doesn't respond or removed? We have huge tasks to know and find ourselves.

Computers, from the first to the second generations used some electric and electronics devices to power the computer and the third generation, used Machine Control Programs (MCP) which was stored into a disc and put into a machine drive and then power the machine with energy to start functioning and respond to other applications.

After this, MCP operating system, many computer companies and individuals designed and released new approach of the computer hardware, Personal Computer (PC)) that would take a smaller office space, yet doing the same or more work than the mainframe computers.

This was the beginning of Disc Operating System (DOS). Although, it was still on disc it could be copied or down loaded into the PC memory; Read Only Memory (ROM) which was then built into the PC. Computer uses another memory as a rough pad for whatever it's assigned to do, called Random Access Memory (RAM). DOS added feathers to its structures by developing window technology.

Some of the computer companies, that joined the race of making and or assembling PCs; IBM, Wang, Apple, Jet, ICL, NCR, etc. This action, saw the decline of the mainframe computer usage. Wang introduced its proposal and usage of paperless office PC, a new birth of scanning and touch technology.

Apple, also went ahead with its user friendly PC and software including the features of the wide area network (WAN) and local area network (LAN), thus setting up the tone of communication network as was seen in the early 2000s. Even before this, a number of computer companies had developed fax machines to copy and send information replacing hand mailing processes.

While WAN and LAN data and information security will remain a challenge as midway hatching may intensify resulting in data and information distortion. Service providers would connect with their clients so that they can have access to these with their gargets at the comfort of their homes or leisure. Even here Eswatini, when we grow up, we tired an empty match box on both ends of a long rope and then talk to each other.

Due to the introduction of WAN and LAN many systems were to re-configure, re-engine, re-design, re-program, re-subroutine, etc., amended to accommodate the emerging communication facilities to the re-systems.

- The dominance of integration in systems design, application and operations gained a momentum during this period of integration. Those who pioneers of putting the ideas computerization and formulating the communicating tools and languages with these machines established a solid foundation of technology that will benefit even the next generations and the e-technology. Due to the power of science and technology these people made it possible for us, users communicate with these objects computers.

THE GENERATION OF COMPUTERS & THEIR OPERATION SYSTEMS :

It be noted that mathematicians played a pivot role in the establishment of computers and computerization before the processes were even recorded as generations; 1940 to 1956 First Generation characterized as vacuum tubes as circuits and magnetic drums for memory, 1956 to 1963 Second Generation known for transistors, 1964 to 1971 Third Generation using Integrated circuits, 1972 to 2010 Fourth Generation known for microprocessors or chips, 2011 to futuristic Fifth Generation known for Artificial Intelligence (AI), silicon and fiber. This is indeed revolutionizing the world and how they do our operations in partnership with machines.

The first, second and third generations of computation had their data input through punching or keying from documented information then producing computer readable input to computer programs. With the advancement of technology and digitalization, new mode of input is expected to further reduce input errors and weak verification controls. Data will come direct from the source and verified in-situ.

So, these machines or semi human kind machines, will not only have the AI, but will have some kind of a commonsense prevailing in society and beyond. The new and advanced technological innovation will influence the known pattern of thinking, executing and analyzing data and information.

This has already been seen that the screens have facilities of being touched, pulled, pushed in all four directions and the screen can accommodate a number of outsides in forward or reverse fashion and condition and the screen pictures may enhance the quality and even the shape of any desired object. This is enhanced by the window technology allowing the screen to show a number of operations, zoomed, minimized and kept in different portions of the screen.

As technology improves, saw some operation systems reducing the involvements of operators and even programmers, the turn key operations, you turn one key and the rest is done by the system or program. This might mean nothing to novices and people who believe in automation, whatever machines do, they are programmed.

- Computerization seem to have gained an upper end in trade and commerce, especially in accessing data and information and providing relevant services in time and affordable manner. These machines and the operating systems have developed friendly usage and communication tools that don't need a lot of skill. The usage of these have brought in a number of advantages; portable, huge memory storage, mobility, reduced office space, work and personal data accessible on request any time, etc.

WITHOUT TIME NO PAST, PRESENT 0R FUTTURE :

The incoming of the year 2000, caused a scare in the recording of the date as information had gained a lot of ground between 1975 and 1999. Even to find the difference between years, one would use DDMMYY – DDMMYY and a number of computer programs and systems had to be amended to treat this in this order DDMMYYYY – DDMMYYYY, Year 2000 also known as Y2K.

Y2K brought in a huge panic in terms of the usage of the date format. Date determines proper functionality of operating systems be their accounting and or information. As the above yy00 and yyyy2000 wouldn't produce the same results but confusion.

Therefore, this demanded a massive systems amendment to avoid loss information which had regenerated into information, communication and technology (ICT). Time is the source of planning, at times you plan for what you are likely to see and appreciate.

If you see tomorrow, the next day and even the future, then you have stopped thinking, your mind is dormant and not capable of meeting challenges and providing solutions. So, time helps and guides one to determine and engage the speed needed to complete the said project or goal.

The old saying that time waits for nobody and that time is money have more meaning now than when these phrases were crafted. You lose time, you lose economic development and prosperity and finally you lose opportunities.

- Only time will guarantee progress and achievement within certain periods of planning and assessment. If you don't have time or even know it, you will never know when to reach your perceived destination. In other words, you will have no goals and vision, thus walking through thick darkness.

WORK AND WORKER LINKED :

With the events and introduction of networks and then interconnection encouraged by village globalization and computer technology, reduced office work into online feature thus enabling work to be done and performed anywhere and anytime rendering the work to follow the workers and vice versa, traceable to perform the duties when demands detect.

This approach reduces office space for operations and probably giving it to boardrooms and conferences and finally encouraging outsourcing of operations or of the non-core business of the company or organization. The importance of a date and time can't be over emphasized, they determine the past, the present and the future, even the identification of days, weeks, months and years.

Sources of data or information since the beginning of computerization has always been offices and people, who will take these to the computers for processing and collect the report back to the office for people to work on them and WAN and LAN had reduced the travelling time of the data or information to the processing centres.

Due to this innovation, fast connectivity on e-operations, e-performance, e-judiciary, e-engineering and e-designs, are expected to be the key captains of the economy, finance, businesses, corporate, government and non-government organizations, machine to machine and no mid-person with papers.

They will e-engine and e-design their operations and performance to meet the e-approach, e-system, e-Operations and e-system conditions. This will need a new approach in executing work and performance, resulting in mobile data and information transmission.

Our traditional ways of thinking and using data and information will upgraded, thus embracing and endorsing new designs without losing our original thinking. Our policies and records to have all information and linked to the national, regional, community and family to data and information.

May be their personal identity number be reviewed and enriched with all information and some conditions and routes to access it. Besides all these, the national network must be universal and accessible to all who need it and the technology innovation available to the wider populace the country and then international.

E-operation and e-system promote fast economic development in this competitive environment and revolution. Safety of all the data and information need care and permanent guarantee of protection against all possibilities of hacking and manipulation of data and information and the need to have a futuristic change of the hardware and software without losing the content of the ROM.

Computerization has become the centre of all operations, thus providing access to information to numerous individuals at the same time, for both good and bad usage, then one needs to understood and care taken on the consequences of disposable data and information. Therefore, ICT encourages users of this technology to clean up their operations to prevent becoming a source of harmful or bad information.

It is about transparency and accountability, thus promoting sustainable economic development. This technology must have road blocks, signs and stops to reduce being the gate way for corruption and money laundering and all associated with them. Many countries have gone into the usage of ICT without modifying their ways of operations, thus giving a chance to wrong element to use and access information.

Others have even accepted and embraced the e-government without disbanding their traditional way of operations. Technology mustn't ignore the communication of the people even in their accepted classification and language. In other words, should accommodate their living style patterns and favorites in both private and public spheres.

Technology mustn't frighten the people but remain a useful tool to easy communication burdens. Therefore, a country mustn't shy away from developing its indigenous communication language or languages if the people desire them.

Then, computer systems will internalize interpretation codes without subjecting the user to do the same. The computer hardware and software must promote and embrace any accepted cultural norms of the community and or populace. There may be a need to develop a commercial language and or for a particular business.

- Both work and workers must have healthy marriage and the investor must provide sustainable relationship love and trust between the two, in order to have top quality products that will conquer the market. In doing this, production must have constant communication to people and vice versa. Electronic components in these machines and systems have facilitated interlinkage of the systems hence now called e-name.

THE THREE PILLARS OF COMPUTERIZATION :

The introduction of computerization mustn't be associated with other conditions, but the three pillars of computerization, that is; speed, accuracy and efficiency (SAE). These aren't the end to themselves, but encourage the shareholders, directors and managers to think and plan for new development of the company or organization. These reports aren't just for shelving, but working tools for expansion.

Computerization on its own can't correct all the wrongs of the operation, but a well analyzed and designed system, specification, operation, data handling and the right personnel can help and promote it to perfection. Computerization shouldn't be treated like fashion or as an identity and class of a particular type of people in society and in places of employment.

There is always the need for people to do things for themselves and or the company, organization, community, etc. Then, the need for health people or technology. In order for these to be productive, the economy must be healthy too. People must be empowered and afforded a space for their on innovation.

The usage of technology in processing our day to day activities involve all types of people; young or old, educated or not, classification or not, social standing or not, etc.

Both the software and hardware mustn't frighten people, but embrace them as they are. It is like wanting to communicate with people that can't understand each other and expect to come out with a bridging language to push their agenda. In this case, the agenda is processing and production of data to produce useful information to assist one to face the prevailing problems and activities of the changing times and environment.

Who should adapt; the technology or the normal at the time? International Telecommunication Union (ITU) has been advocating for Digital Migration (DM) and free universal access to such facilities. Unfortunately, ITU conditions are only directed to the leadership, leaving the people only as consumers.

A number of these gate ways are handled by governments and people mayn't have a health communications with governments, thus delaying benefiting to the DM. Some mayn't even see that they aren't connected to the DM in a long time because of using the smooth terrain of potholes, an intensive treatment unity, indeed. If your television set is still connected to an air-real, then you haven't migrated and you aren't benefiting from digitalization.

- What next after all the goodies on your golden table? Is it being greedy? Whether the usage is in computerization, electronic involvement, the 4th industrial revolution or artificial intelligence the main issue is SAE.

SELF-CONTAINED OPERATIONS AND SYSTEMS :

The hardware and software shouldn't be only highly efficient, but extremely friendly, thus ignoring the literacy of the user or client. The architecture and specification must embrace and endorse a high spirit of AI. These systems will lead the person using the machine to the desired target or if completely lost, take that person to the end and then allow a proper start, thus not allowing the operation to enter into and endless loop. The hardware and software, mustn't be subjected into freezing, but must end the operation and display the sudden ending and restart condition.

These are user friendly routings which have all relevant messages. No user of technology garget must be stacked in front of the screen without knowing what to do.

They are moving to machines and operations that will have a sense of recognizing analogy and or digital functions and operations and convert where necessary. Are these machines and operations going to replace human beings? Or are these machines going to design operations within themselves without the knowledge of the original designers?

Human beings themselves are in a better position to answer these questions, but the truth is that some human beings will be replaced by these and a number of human beings will be consumers. This may reduce the common saying that reports are gathering dust in government offices.

It might be a question of misfiling data and or information. Or are we saying that within the human being race there would be some super people in the Fourth Industrial Revolution (4IR) and beyond, thus creating some form of Artificial Brains (AB) and even hands? Some, knowingly or unknowingly will reduce themselves into that level.

This isn't new, they come from colonization and slavery, especially in Africa. They are still complaining in their comfort zones; caves and hideouts and not ready to face the claws of 4IR and AI. Other continents are already working hard on the 4IR and AI and even crafting policies and regulations on these.

When the 4IR and AI are in full swing, human beings, will now concentrate on challenging issues to usher in perfect life as designed and specified by God. In doing all these, there is a need to craft and or amend their existing laws to accommodate the operation of (AB) or hands and the concept of the 4IR. Technology is advancing and promoting new ideas with infinity industrial revolution that will soon expose the Original Intelligence (OI), ushering a new beginning.

- Hands off approach is upon them as human beings and self-determination is extended to all operation entities. This changes and challenges are bound to create divisions within the human being race; those with skills to develop AI systems and the users and true with 4IR, leaving behind a huge number of people in the ocean of ignorance. Very interesting indeed, machine through science and technology developing commonsense through electronic tools.

OPPORTUNITIES IN THE SKY :

With this new approach in operations and doing business, they will explore, as a nation, their air space for business opportunities assisted by the innovation of advancement and technology. In ushering these new opportunities, their current status quo, in everything they do and live by must be understood by all the people, not just the architects and engineers of the 4IR and AI innovations.

Some of the 4IR and AI tools if not all, come through advance learning and research, issues that can't be achieved in a short space of time. History can confirm that many poor countries, especially in Africa, are under developed, their plans and even usage of their tools to craft them, hence remain in a copycat format.

While the 4IR is gaining ground and momentum, ahead of AI implementation. It isn't clear, as to how will the fundamental tools of developing application software will be liberalized to provide independent innovation. Advance technology has always subjected those who wanted to use it to move away from their comfort zone to the technology towers and expose themselves to new environment, tools, communication, languages, etc. Africa seem to be lacking behind in this advancement.

It is hoped that the 4IR and AI will usher in tools that have options that suit the interest of the users of technology, but with an acceptable international standards. As previously stated, technology is here to change our life style and how best will we access information; sense, touch, see, sound and sign language and technology will get information in a logical manner and even validate and verify its origin, thus reducing and eliminating fake data of information.

Due, to this demand, no human being must be devoid of OI. These issues or conditions that will no longer attract questions but AI. Both OI and AI will need human beings to reconnect to their past and the future, even the future itself. Who can't want to know the events of the nine months before birth?

- Technology advancement has opened more horizons to enhance life in the sky above our environment not only for residential but leisure and food security. Due to science and technology, there are opportunities for countries to expand their boundaries in a meaningful way in the sky above their soil area.

THE FUTURE BEFORE THE FUTURE :

As entering into this terrain, what must be key to watch and probably master to survive? Or they are burying our past and replacing it with the unknown new normal or even in prison of the past problems? The future can't be crafted from no base or even the zeal for wanting more, not just being greedy.

The physical body appearance of anything isn't the issue, will still be there, but with numerous ways to access, use, recycle, receive, store, any option of one's choice in his or her fingertips. Well, one can be there without being there, information will flow and follow them at their comfort zones to function and have access to whatever they need. The introduction of the AI and AB is pointing at a new relationship between human beings and machines as friends and colleagues, not just tools.

This is a challenge of having information that you may fail to fully utilize. Will, their minds cope with the so much flow of information? That is, likely to invade One's privacy or the equation of public and privacy, would need a review due to the demand of the economy and service delivery?

Most of us are familiar with the tiredness of the physical body. It is expected, that laws of employment and company files will need amendment to protect the multi processes that may have access to their data and information.

While science and technology are fast improving, new and innovation challenges are gaining momentum too, influenced by the shortages of raw materials. Due to this, science and technology must reposition themselves into recycling. This could include reusable technics.

With this science and technology, they should see the future before the future itself, thus guaranteeing sustainable projects and actions to be taken in due course. Technology is pointing at a direction of embracing the origin of our thinking power and what they are capable of? Their environment and up bringing have reduced our potential of seeing the future and its consequences.

- The period of recycled origin and environment has surfaced, without realizing that there is nothing new, but it is how scenarios emerge and act to provide solutions to current challenges. Isn't strange that technology can reveal the future way before the future itself.

THE HUMAN RECORD IN A CHIP :

Where are the 4IR, AI and Science & Technology in general leading the world to; semi human beings tools, super human beings machines or robot controlled environment? The introduction of virtual usage proved that human beings can be there, yet not physically there. Who would dispute that pictures and even interviews are destined to be conducted virtually?

Geographical physical systems (GPS) and all corners of the world can easily be located and the current happening captured. Individuals throughout the world are now introduced into personal codes and countries have their codes for identification and location, that is, people and their locations without them knowing.

Normal, strange and unbecoming happenings will be identified and people immediately informed of their happening within a specific time and duration. Indeed, the world is moving towards interesting times with fascinating opportunities and challenges.

Due to the chips that would be imbedded into human beings or animals bodies for easy access to the details and historical background of our lives, be it health, profession or any useful information needed by the state and security agencies. These bodies, from time to time hid their veins, thus delaying an emergence of blood transfusion.

Science and technology have already provided solution to this, search and find the vein on a suitable spot and then put a chip called pot. It isn't only to think outside the box but understand the environment for sustainable development and seeing far beyond technology. There can't be a static time and space. There are too many things to expose before the end of life time.

- One's life record stored in the body and to trace one's

movement and type of sicknesses, medical treatment and all necessary details to enable quick response in case of emergencies thus affording help just-in-time. Clearly information is more important than the problem or sickness.

PRIVACY UNKNOWINGLY EXPOSED TO THE PUBLIC :

When the personal identity number (PIN) card was introduced, it looked simple but it stores far reaching information on them as people. The question is, are people ready to surrender their all information to the state? Or is the state willing to fully inform the populace why it needs so much information about the populace?

As it has already been revealed that information is within the tip of our fingers, not long, it will be your thoughts that has been detected by the intelligent machine, one has approached or next to it, even, stripe one naked without knowing.

Changing from one operation to another require new approaches, regulations and even laws. Currently, technology isn't universally accessible to those who might need it. This gap will continue to widen and disadvantage a bigger population of the world. There are those who had everything at their disposals including owning airplanes and concords to enable them to attend Meetings and Summits in convenient times and environments.

Unfortunately, many of such Meetings and Summits from 2021 are conducted virtually and no more need to fly to places of these Meetings and Summits. The question is, what will these powerful machines and gorgeous conference centres, now do? Many leaders and managers have been combining these Meetings and Summits with tourism and leisure at the expense of their countries and companies.

Well, these will be used for tourism, leisure, entertainment, etc., and transport for goods to facilitate online shopping. Now, one can imagine running a seminar, meeting, conference, courses and even lunch on and leisure on board airplane flying around the country airspace without landing for whatever time, even spend nights there or the airplane stop midair.

This approach will enable leaders to know their country boundaries, beauty of the land and the valleys. And this approach will encourage the usability of the country airspace that has been dormant for a long time. What will stop the airspace from creating dwelling facilities, because the airspace engineering and architecting are already with us?

Will, the airspace be commercialized, when these futuristic approaches are implemented? If this will be the norm, will the laws and or regulations be crafted to give guidance of the operation of the airspace?

Talk of AI, these semi human beings tools, will they be like, being taught, not only to process data, but to check logic and values of the issues at hand? This is bound to introduce new approaches in solving and providing new sustainable solutions to benefit local and international communities and societies.

The world is moving to the unknown, but with hope and determination that the future is brighter than both the past and the current, period. Science and technology are playing the leading role and influencing all sectors of communities and societies, rich or poor to move on because the horizon is reachable.

Some people keep dogs as a security tool, but these dogs can't report the happenings, then the dog must be equipped with a camera so that when it is bucking, should trigger the gargets to take a picture and sound of the object. Then, dogs will be the powerful property security keepers.

With technology, who should worry about commercial roads where trucks are torched, put the smart gargets that will monitor all the activities of those roads with facilities to report to the nearest police station, country wild, owners of those trucks.

- With technology and its innovation there is no place to hid, hence must always be cleared as if going to a competition, that is, the nature of this technological emancipation. Can the airspace above the surface of the soil being commercially used for individually basis.

VIRUS AND VACCINES OR ACCESSSIBLE & AFFORDABILITY :

With the emerging of the 4IR and the vaccine development as a profitable and sustainable business of the post COVID 19, pose a groom future for the countries that have been known as poor or underdeveloped. How can these countries, suddenly find themselves with the skills, machines and technology to produce these vaccines for their populace? Is Africa again missing the opportunity to be a standalone continent, thus reducing dependence on handouts and donations targeted at only consumption?

When the COVID 19 Pandemic showed its ugly head at the end of 2019 and in other parts of the world and poor nations early 2020, medical and vaccine gurus cried with one voice; that is, it is a new virus and there is no vaccine for it and it takes time to produce a new vaccine. They were all schooled on this, just after mid2020, there was a possibility of a vaccine and later vaccines came and attracting huge prices. As usual, poor countries couldn't raise the needed funds, had to queue for funds and the donated vaccines.

Immediately after this, a new demand for poor countries to produce vaccines for their citizens, hence the World Trade Organization (WTO) was asked to issue a temporary waiver to produce COVID 19 vaccines. The World Health Organization (WHO) gave the green light to those countries interested in producing these vaccines to proceed without the WTO approval. All these are United Nation organs, but why this war? What will be the protection of those who will be vaccinated by these locally produced vaccines?

Technology transfer remains a missing link for many individuals and countries. The gap between the rich and the poor nations seem to be widened rendering the poor ones as perpetual consumers of finished and polished products and goods. At times receiving and using unprotected vaccines from unrecognized suppliers.

What are chances of Africa, indeed African countries localizing software and hardware, applications and equipment with international flavor and compete in the world markets in producing vaccines? Or are they still going to be controlled by the principles of the survivor of the fittest and the declarations and policies of whatever world groups want? Promises by these groups have always been there but based on selfish benefits, since the era of colonization.

Will the new approach for equality work or apply the wait while the poor nations are in recovery processes to come to the level of the developed world? The issue at hand is technology transfer, the quality of that transfer and the skills of using it under the prevailing conditions of poor countries, especially in the African continent.

- Will the body be able to develop its own virus to defend itself against any harmful viruses that may invade the body? As if science and technology are only influencing certain items of the living, it is hoped that human being bodies will acquire the same skill and produce stronger defense virus to fight the anti-human being viruses.

THE CONNECTIVITY OF THE LEADER & THE LEAD :

World leaders need to deliberate on, yes, important issues but whatever they resolve never reach the people. In fact, the people never have direct input to all these resolutions. They aren't part to the origins of these deliberations. The world needs energy to produce the so many items demanded by the economy and the current energy has its source from heat and heat isn't a bosom friend of climate change.

What are chances of generating energy from cold? There is no debate and doubt about the harm of climate change, but are the world leaders willing to abandon supremacy, profits and the huge equipment investment?

Now, talk about new investment and skills which mayn't be easily available due to a number of issues, including new type of engineers and scientists and materials to generate energy from cold. Or say that solid materials are the future and that flexible materials are remote and no space in life?

With the advancement of science and technology, a chance of flexible materials is possible for these to carry heavy materials and life will be fascinating due the popularization of satellite and wind engineering.

Will, this be the end of petroleum products and all associated with it? It may look impossible, but science and technology innovation disagree with that accession but render them as challenges. The world should fight climate change with technological tools not just speeches and conventions.

In order to develop beyond handouts and donations, there is a need of an education system that will empower the people to think and plan beyond the foreseeable future. If there is a believe that the usage of certain minerals produce harmful emissions that contribute to the climate change, then should abandon those and replace them with friendly minerals to produce our energy, especially poor country.

Many developed countries can use any of these minerals that are the cause of climate change because they have enough funds and resources to mitigate any disaster due to climate change effect, thus causing less harm an option not possible developing and underdeveloped countries.

Challenges of the future must be sorted out, not in the future but currently in order to avoid uncertainty. The failure of leadership and the populace to be proactive have resulted in the panic caused by unknown viruses and attacks.

Will Africa be equal to the other continents within the foreseeable future? It's known that the developed world is promising technology and skill transfer and probably materials. Bear in mind, that, this is the competitive and survivor of the fittest environment. It's clear, if redesigning of the said technology will be allowed to reduce and eliminate the cancer of permanent dependence.

Trade on its nature demands dominance, favorable advantage, bigger share in the market, hence some sort of secrecy on the production of the products. So, it is easy to pronounce pledges and promises, but business is known to have volunteered to put itself into an inferior competitor resulting into the loss of the market power of that competitor.

- There are commonalities in any environment, be it at work and or social life will be inseparable and will have nothing to hide. Therefore, it's important to allow free flow of data and information.

NO SIGNS OR INDICATORS :

Those in leadership are promising equal opportunities, normal life style for all but fall short of indicating how these goodies would be sustained even introduced. People are indoctrinated into believing that perfect life style will take place in the prescribed years but never notice that those making such promises will not be in leadership or dead, to clear the promised elusions and even oversee the implementations of those promises.

Life is about independence, to promote equitable trade and competition encourage the survivor of the fittest. People have visions and missions or goals; guided or not and must have access to opportunities with some protection. Is this possible if not, why not?

How genuine are these promises of equality when the world isn't flat but round, implying that there is climbing the hill and going down the slope and at times, going horizontal, thus setting up different conditions and achievements? As they speak the gap between the haves and haven't is widening and there are no signs or indicators that it is on the decrease. Or is it a question of telling people what they want to hear and cultivating hope that will never see the light of the following day?

Many countries, mainly in Africa have two living standards; rich and poor, standing at 10 per cent and ninety per cent and there is no known source of how these become so rich in the ocean of poverty. It is envisaged that technology if introduced to all the people of a country, especially in the so called poor countries, it can create the missing level, where these people will learn to stand alone restore their dignity, thus reducing the handouts syndrome that has subjected people to think and accept that they were destined to remain poor.

- It is easier said than done, they talk of poverty, inequality and even the future happiness but no signs and indicators of how these can be put behind the present and future generation. It is the gap between the haves and haven't, especially if the source of their earnings is the same.

THE HARM OF ENDLESS DEPENDENCE :

Trillion Aires and Billionaires of this world are exploring life in the universe while majority of the world populace are struggling to put food on the table and diseases are having field day in their bodies. Countries are still classified as developed, developing and poor or underdeveloped thus continue to group themselves according to their status and then decide their future.

First world countries and the other nations haven't disbanded their donation spirits, especially to the African continent, but still short of genuine empowerment. Will Africa ever stop to be on the receiving side or be the donator to the other continents that are in need? This will put the continent as an equal to the other continents.

History seem to suggest that the origin of technology as they see it to date started in Africa. But, why is Africa trailing far behind all the continents in technological innovation? Could this be by design or just the weakness of the African leadership? So much work needs to be done in the continent by both leadership and the lead.

The building of Pyramids in Egypt, making of military weapons like spears and knives of all parts, communication using strings, making shoes using plants outer skin, medicine, etc., to advance development, started in Africa. Technology shouldn't be used to create division but to enhance improved service to human kind. What is perceived to be impossible must be made possible because mind potentials are limitless only the environment is blocking the imagination.

In life, certain needs expand and others decrease implying that they have to use technology to effectively balance the equation. Does this mean that certain essentials must be stopped or abandoned? Technology is necessary to help mitigate those problems. The size of a country mustn't determine the advancement of technology but the quality of life is paramount.

- If one can't stand up and defend his or her status will remain an underdog forever, probably a permanent consumer. There is hope that rich or poor, Africans will learn to invest in technological innovation in order to spearhead the sustainable economic development that is destined to compete with the demands of the civilized world.

TOURISM IN-SITU AND AT NEEDS :

The distances between points of needs mustn't deter service delivery. Tourism and leisure may remain dominant in travelling and exploring the beauty of nature as it stands. This is in no way preventing virtual travelling. There would be no need to be in Eswatini to travel to the corners of the country, to view the beautiful mountains, hills, valleys, cliffs and gorges of; Kwendzeni, Mahhoshe, Hhoro, Lufafa, Ngwavuma, cliffs; Mtsambama, Mavukutfu, Bhulungwane, Nkhaba, Mliba, hills; eNgudze, Sigwe, Hluti, Phunga, Lubobmo, Mdzimba, Sinceni, mountains; Shiba's Breast, Gobholo, Timpisini, valleys; Phophonyane, Mahamba, Luhlazana, gorges.

This is tourism in the comfort of one's home and or space, due to technology innovation. People in these areas can show case the beauty of the hidden places in the country, thus creating opportunities for local and international tourism. .

The land scope of the country must be virtually designed to allow current movement to be exposed to tourism. As a country, what does this mean? New technological design skills needed or necessary to provide current status of an area or environment. In this, the country will enhance the identification types of plantations, vegetables, fruits, indigenous trees and grasses, even types of wildlife animals in these specific areas.

This will also enable other services to be rendered remotely, imagine conducting court processes where the judge, the prosecutor, defense lawyer and applicant aren't in the same place. Accordingly, this will help speed up justice service delivery to benefit irrespective of location and environment conditions.

They are moving into new design tools. This technological innovation would recall the original picture and or environment and assimilate the current zooming or viewing. As a Swazi nation, we must position ourselves to virtually draw our country to compete in virtual tourism of the virtual world.

What would this mean, to a country that is developing and has been captured by the dependence syndrome? Our education and training would need a drastic overhaul to meet the new environment of the future and beyond. We are moving to a terrain where every move one enjoys will be exposed for all to see, meaning that hooliganism will have no space in society.

The security that is provided by dogs will not just be baking, as it bakes, a picture of the intruder will be taken with all relevant information of the visitor. Those shops who have installed CCVs in their shops can attest that stealing has been reduced and some instances eliminated. It is a known fact, that people who steal or intend to and or want to do wrong don't want to be seen.

What is common with people that are prone to breaking the law is darkness without any recognized entity on sight, so technology becomes handy to clear the ambiguity, it will hid there but see and record everything. Now you can imagine writing in the air instead on a surface as seen in the rainbow. How about a verbatim message that can be printed as if it was written, technology on the move.

- They see and touch items they have never physically seen and touched, they have become tourist but physically and mentally sitting in one environment, the world hasn't only become a global village, but their small rooms and kitchens. There is no dispute that technology innovation is reducing the globe into accessibility to all human beings and the living organisms. The hidden or undiscovered treasure of the universe will soon be in the public domain for everyone to appreciate and enjoy.

NETWORK & INFORMATION MOBILITY :

The innovation that is coming with the usage technology in putting the request is fascinating, physical touching or sensing, talking or using sign language. Very interesting and challenging, the keys in these tools are becoming too small and the tip of their fingers are the size of two keys, suggesting that we will need to design an artificial tip of the finger that will be used to touch the keys.

As if this isn't the end of surprises in this technology innovation, that is, talking to the software and hardware. This will be another dilemma, where the language, tone and level of pronouncing those words must be designed to provide uniformity.

Technology especially in communication and transport is moving us into situations where services in these operands will be revolving in drone's usage, not just for goods but the needs of artificial people that will be in position to deliver verbatim as opposed the network connectivity.

It be noted that when one uses network services the messages or secrets, the gargets might have no power to control even a guarantee that the original will reach the destination in the same form and quality. Who, currently would doubt the effect and strength of hacking and corruption via network connectivity?

- Wow, information no longer following those who need it, its resident in them hence available at a twingicle of an eye within the touch of a key even speech or engaging the device. And at times maybe accessible to other entities, thus making this information available to all those you are connected to.

SAFETY OF ORIGINAL INFORMATION :

They can't guarantee safety and hacking, hence there is a need for a system that will not only check the safety of the transmission route, but will fight any intruder and even satisfies itself that the receiving site is fully protected against any attack. Currently, the software has a guarantee that the transmitted document or information is similar to the original one. These systems will in turn develop something similar to what is called DNA in human beings. Any document or information must be traceable of its original source and even report on its current spot.

While in this crusade of technology advancement, they are aware that technology can be used to reduce wrong doing because as time goes on nothing will hid from technology, yet they know wrong doing is done behind the scene in hiding or darkness.

One can imagine that when travelling you are scanned before you start moving and continue being checked if it is conforming to the original approved safety conditions. Human beings with the help of technology will soon enjoy their full potential on earth as designed by the Creator. They will make sub human beings to do things for us.

They all know and believe that to err is human, then how would we define this when dealing with Al, especially when the issue at hand is between the AI machine and the human being? What if this AI machine errs or should this be referred to as AI human being?

Will this approach create AI that has capacity to create their own sub-routes to perform certain functions within the main operations? Now, they will need new laws, regulations, safety and privates that might be created by the inter-reaction between AI and AI human beings.

The world is in search of perfection and the Centre of this work is technology. Technology itself needs tools that are futuristic to prevent any chance of errors and or malfunctioning.

- Are machines going to develop some kind of DNA to identify the parenthood or source of originality of information even data? This could help reduce hacking and stealing of information because of this facility of revealing the path undertaken to reach whatever destination. Those who may have shared, read, commented and the created influence that data or information would have created in society. And one wonders how these new approaches will be legally understood?

MACHINE TO MACHINE OPERATIONS :

They are approaching an era where machines or machines like human beings will take a Centre stage for operations due to the advancement of technology in AI. This will not only demand the e-recondition our way of thinking, but will usher in new e-policies, e-laws, e-regulations and how these are implemented and monitored and by who, probably themselves. It be noted that the usage of AI will finally benefit human beings, then must understand the e-processes. This may look like fiction, but will soon reveal itself as the reality.

One can imagine, these minded machines checking each other and even re-sequencing and prioritizing of execution of some projects. This means that common sense will no longer only afforded to human beings, but minded machines too.

Well, how will human beings control and or monitor common sense articulated by these new branded human face machines? What if these commit mistakes or break the law and or e-laws? Even before thinking of crafting the laws and regulations, we should be considering e-judiciary to navigate malfunction of e-machines, including e-policing, e-prosecution and e-investigation.

They need to be reminded that at the dawn of computerization, even here Eswatini, people feared being replaced by machines, but now these human beings like machines will actually do the real job without being assisted by human beings. Technology usage innovation has always been on speed, accuracy and efficiency.

This means that human beings will have at their disposal enough information and time to plan and research for the future needs. What about the fear of technology encroaching into the personal life of people, without any request? Those who travel are familiar with this?

- Is the advancement of science and technology challenging the capability and power of human beings? Then, what is the future of human beings intelligence or is it a question of human beings developing some tools that will phase them out? Isn't strange that human beings somehow depict the machine component suggesting that there is a potter that knows the mixture, quality and durability of the product?

UNCERTAINTY OF FUTURE DOMINION :

Even before, they start thinking of the 5lR, they must imagine one person controlling these robotic machines to perform certain operations at the same time, thus eliminating any waiting time to assembly a product to the required standard. Eventually to a condition where these robotic machines will have an exclusive domain in manufacturing and assembling.

Are human beings again going to be caught unaware of what technology and innovation are taking them to? As the people in whatever region or part of world, must prioritize research and development. The future mustn't come, as a surprise, but probability of disaster must be exposed in order to prepare for those eventualities.

Not so distance future, they will be talking of e-electronic and e-future in the comfort of e-living e-conditions. This should be better understood by bringing the life style of transporting messages from one place to another and even how writing started. They give the transporter an object with symbols to tell the content of the message.

At times, they would write; on a mud soil and let it dry UP, on the soil and the transporter to sing those letters until reaching the destination, on a slate, on card board like paper, on paper and ICT came out with the new tools that will usher in e-ICT.

Although technology has advanced into this level, there people in the world, including their leadership that are still glued into the usage of papers. This is a confirmation that AI will create different layers of how people think and execute their daily activities.

- The future is coming up with a number of unmeasurable challenges. The future is far yet near due to availability of information at the instance touching the key board of whatever electronic device. At times information come to us without any request, hence learning and exposed to data and information to improve our own lives. Are human beings ready for these changes, time will tell?

COMMENT :

Who said that a computer or other gargets of technology must be designed and used according cultures of other people and their environments? Being an indigenous Swazi I can't lay down my nets and operate my computer and other gargets of technology without problems because of the designs of these gargets. Currently, these are made to demand other tools; tables, chairs and all associated with the culture and environment of where they were designed and assembled. Can one imagine a computer or cell phone in a shell of our local trees (umvangati or uncweba) wood, properly cut into thin panels. These type of trees produce strong timber that resist easy wearing up or decay.

Can you imagine a computer system to respond in SiSwati to guarantee universal access to technology to all without being compelled into learning some kind of characters, codes or language in order to access technology goodies? This will enhance knowledge for all irrespective of age, upbringing, part or environment of the world, poor or rich.

As an individual, in a country that mayn't have enough resources to meet all the educational needs of people to advance themselves, but it is a hope and faith that one day, will produce national space engineers, astronauts and other technologists that will have the zeal to explore the bottom of the ocean, be part to world exploration programs.

Other countries of the world are investing so much in technology to explore the untapped opportunities in the universe. People were never invited to come colonize Africa, they mobilized their resources and built ships and then sailed to Africa and indeed discovered opportunities, which later were used to influence Africans to abandon their life styles and indigenous knowledge.

It is the same people that haven't stopped exploring the world including the ecosystem of the oceans and Africa is watching or probably complaining about the effects of colonization, with no strategy on training to empower their citizens to be in these teams that are exploring the world. They don't see Africa taking the initiative to be part to these programs.

Even if African countries can't afford to have units in their governments to handle these advancements, but can have their trained citizens working with those countries that are moving to the unknown opportunities. Who says, we can't find life in the sun and even live in the other planets? Technology and information have unlimited opportunities for those who are eager to know the unknown and discover the undiscovered and face new challenges in life.

DEDICATION :

My late first born daughter Hlengiwe Penelope. When I joined computerization she wasn't there and only came in my entrenched life in the knowledge and spirit of using computers. Being my first born daughter, played a trick in my mind and spiritual rhyme. My two older sisters died before, I was born. Even at her early age she was like my sister, hence I continued calling her my sister until her death. As it is noticed, I was one of the first Swazis to join then this uncommon profession in the country.

Don't miss out!

Visit the website below and you can sign up to receive emails whenever Shongwe Mbho publishes a new book. There's no charge and no obligation.

https://books2read.com/r/B-A-VKIEB-TPLPG

BOOKS 2 READ

Connecting independent readers to independent writers.

Also by Shongwe Mbho

Dancing in the Middle of a Marriage Storm
The intricacies in eswatini
tibongo netinanatelo
Emeswati Abetsini Atsini
Innovation and emancipation of computerization

About the Author

Mbho Shongwe: A liberal Democrat that embraces human rights and cultural and traditional norms, especially those of the Swazi nation. Without forcing people on religious ideology but marriage is a common factor. Am a Christian and subscribe to justice, fairness, peace and self determination. The rule of law is a guarantee for respect to all and culture and tradition must endorse the principles of life. Have experienced the combination of civil and traditional marriage and their good and evil. Had hands on in a number of traditional events and rituals. I divorced, married, widower and with God guidance working to start a new life.

About the Publisher

Lack of knowledge is the ill of the world. Information isn't moving fast to reach people, hence the populace is battling with endless problems; conflicts and wars, due to ignorance. Sharing information through publishing can reduce and finally eliminate the scourge currently faced by the world, thus usher in safety, security and peace for all.

www.ingramcontent.com/pod-product-compliance
Lightning Source LLC
LaVergne TN
LVHW090430210926
848480LV00002B/770
9798230963936